Interior Design

*Make Your Home
Look Amazing!*

*Luxurious Home Decorating
on a Budget*

Table of Contents

Introduction

Interior design is crucial in making your home as aesthetically pleasing as possible. Even the slightest knowledge about interior decorating on a budget can help improve the look of your home and allow it to showcase your unique personality. If you do not have any knowledge about interior design, don't stress - This book will help you every step of the way. You may not be sure exactly what you want either. This is also fine, we'll be here to guide you through the process of designing a unique practical space that your friends will envy.

It is important to note that interior design does not only cover the physical look of your home's interiors. It also plays a major role in improving the functionality of its different parts. Note that even the biggest house will be at risk of losing substantial amount of space if it has poorly designed interiors. It is also possible to transform a small apartment into a cozy and spacious living space by just choosing the right interior design. In other words, interior design is the key to making the most out of the space that you have.

If you want to design your home's interiors without overly exceeding your budget, then make sure to consider important factors like functionality and practicality. This means that any fixtures or accessories that you plan to add into your home should be functional and practical. The items should not only improve the attractiveness of your home, but make it more functional as well. You also need to do careful planning. Coordinate your desired decorations with your family and ask for suggestions. Remember that you will be spending money over the design, so choose wisely so you won't end up wasting your money for a poor choice.

You may find it hard to determine the kind of design that specifically suits your lifestyle and needs since majority of the designs at present do not reveal the need to make alterations, adjustments or improvements until you start to use them. Aside from taking care of the layout, we will also help you in choosing the best lighting, color and decoration for your home.

This book is crafted in such a way that you will know more about the field and the vital factors and aspects revolving around it. With the knowledge that you will gain from this book, you can easily coordinate your wants to your chosen interior designer, making it possible to really get the home that you like.

With the aid of this book, you can easily make a choice as to the elements that should go in each part of your home. This makes it possible for you to contribute a lot in building a functional and appealing home that showcases your unique personality.

Chapter 1: What Makes a Home Visually Appealing?

Your home is the only place where you can find solace after a stressful day at work or after dealing with a lot of familial responsibilities. This is where you can seek comfort and find the kind of peace that you are longing to achieve. It is for this reason that you have to make your home as visually appealing and comfortable as possible. You have to pay close attention to its interior decorations to ensure that it turns out to be the place that you want it to be.

The good news is that you do not have to spend a fortune to decorate your home. By just learning about the things that can make a home visually appealing, you will be able to create one that specifically meets your preferences. The following are just some of the many things that can make a home truly attractive.

Lighting and Fixtures

In interior designing, the right lighting and fixture choices can make a huge difference when planning to achieve an aesthetically pleasing output. Bright lights are good choices especially if you want your home to look more spacious. Invest in good lighting fixtures and fittings so that even the gloomiest part of your home will receive ample light. You should also place the lighting fixtures in strategic places and allow natural light to seep in.

If you want to enhance the look and elegance of your home, then consider adding soft lights. Avoid the use of harsh lighting except in the bathroom and kitchen where such type of lighting fixture is necessary. The lighting fixtures should also perfectly suit the place where you intend to install them.

Relaxing Atmosphere

You can also make your home look more attractive by ensuring that it has a relaxing atmosphere. Make sure that your chosen interior design is relaxing enough and can help you achieve your desired peace of mind. Place all your desired features and designs in the right places so they do not clog up the space. Make your home as comfortable and as relaxing as possible by putting and installing everything in the right places.

Colors and Decorations

Matching the right colors is one of the most crucial aspects in interior design. Choose just one wrong color and it will have a drastic effect on the overall look of a part of your home. When choosing the colors to use in your home, think positive thoughts. This will allow you to choose colors that will bring in a more positive vibe inside your home.

It is also advisable to think about your chosen theme. The colors that you should choose for the different parts and rooms of your home including the kitchen, bedroom, bathroom and living room should perfectly blend with the overall theme. Use your creativity when choosing colors and matching them.

Flower arrangements and wall decorations can also add appeal into your home. If you plan to add wall decorations, then consider hiring professional painters since they can do a better job in producing the best output. You also have the choice to paste wallpapers in the walls of your home. Just make sure that you develop a well-laid out plan to avoid ruining the final output.

Flowers can also make your home more attractive. The right flower arrangements placed in the right places can cheer up everyone inside your home while also leaving an impression of freshness and cleanliness.

Chapter 2: The Core #1 Fundamental Rule for Interior Design

A well-decorated interior plays a crucial role in developing the kind of atmosphere that you want your home to showcase. This is the main reason why careful planning is essential when designing your home's interiors. You have to choose an interior design, which is unique and attractive enough that it can show people your distinct personality as well as the personalities of the people living there.

The fundamental rule in interior designing is to focus on functionality, quality and personality rather than on quantity. This rule is where you can further apply the "less is more" principle. To understand this rule better, here are 3 main principles closely associated to it.

Principle #1 - Functionality

Interior design does not only encompass eye appeal. It also covers aspects that can make a specific room work for you. This means that aside from aesthetics, interior decorating also puts a lot of emphasis on functionality. In ensuring that your home becomes truly functional, you have to think about its focal point. The focal point is the specific place in your home where the eyes travel right after entering.

Examples of focal points include a built-in bookshelf, bay window that has a view and a fireplace. If a room in your home does not come with a natural focal point yet, then it is advisable to create one using a colorful rug or an eye-catching piece of art. Another thing to consider when improving the functionality of your home through interior designing is choosing the right furniture and fixtures. Find out if a piece of furniture fully meets the functions and requirements that you intended for a specific room before buying it.

It is also crucial to choose lighting based not only on visual appeal, but also on the room's functions. Note that each task needs a different light. For instance, you may need indirect lights that tend to simply brighten a specific room for watching TV or for cozy conversations. Accent lighting such as recessed spotlights and track lighting are also perfect choices especially if you plan on enhancing the details, color and texture of a room.

Your desired functionality is also achievable with the right furniture arrangement. A wise tip in effectively arranging your furniture pieces is to mark and measure switches and electrical outlets, doors, windows and vents. It is also advisable to measure furniture pieces and include them in your floor plan. Your major furniture pieces should be in a position that directs to the focal point. This can keep main traffic areas open.

Principle #2 - Personality

Another vital principle in interior designing is integrating your unique personality into it. This is possible through accessorizing. Accessories that you can add into your home's interiors include pictures, area rugs, pillows and vases. These are vital parts of an impressive interior decorating plan. Just make sure that your chosen accessories support the overall theme of your home while also giving more room for flexibility.

To bring out your unique personality and show it in your home's interior decorations, consider adding unique accessories on walls, furniture, mantels, floors and tabletops. You can also hang photos and paintings in your wall.

Principle #3 - Mood / Atmosphere

Your choice of colors, your chosen accessories, amount of pattern and texture, as well as the styles that you have chosen for furnishings can create the kind of mood or atmosphere that you want for a room. In creating the right mood, you have to think about a number of things, so it is best to establish a theme that will serve as your inspiration when formulating decisions.

Setting the right mood when designing a room is also possible by carefully considering vital factors including the theme, inspiration piece, patterns, color cues, furniture items and texture.

Chapter 3: Our 5 Step Guide to Makeover Any Room

Are you planning to give any room in your home its much needed makeover? If your answer is yes, then the 5-step room makeover guide in this chapter can be a huge help for you.

Step #1: Choose a New Theme

The first step in giving a room its much needed makeover is to choose a new theme for it. Carefully plan the theme. It should perfectly fit with your personality and your specific preferences. Deciding on a theme also requires you to figure out color schemes. Avoid choosing your favorite colors because there is a great chance that you will lose your interest in them over time.

If possible, go for colors that you know you have enjoyed for the most part of your life. You should also be flexible when picking a color. The main reason is that you may change your decision once you visit a paint shop and start buying the needed supplies. Your chosen theme and color should be able to create the kind of atmosphere that you want a particular room to create.

Step #2: Paint

Once you have decided the color scheme and the theme, it is time to shop for the supplies needed for painting. Just make sure to clean the room and remove all the clutter before starting to use your purchased supplies. If the room already has an existing paint but you plan on repainting it, then make sure to get a primer.

Primer refers to a white paint that you can use to prepare your wall for the painting job. This can also help prevent the previous paint color from showing up once the new one is already applied.

Another tip when shopping is to try paint samples. You should also take the time to put your preferred or chosen colors together. This can help you figure out if the colors perfectly blend with each other.

Keep in mind that there is a great possibility that you will change your mind regarding color schemes once you start buying the needed supplies and visualizing the potential result. Once you have all the needed supplies, clean up the room that needs the makeover. Use plastic, newspapers or cardboard to cover the floor to prevent the paint from messing up your flooring or carpet.

The next step is to start painting. Just make sure to do it with caution. Utilize rollers for huge and open areas. You can then use a brush to paint the edges, corners and trim of the walls. Use your creativity when doing the job by painting unique and attractive patterns such as stripes and polka dots.

Step #3: Accessorize

A room makeover will never be complete without adding the right accessories into it. Accessorizing is a vital component in any interior designing or room makeover project. For instance, if you are planning to reorganize your bedroom, then accessories like picture frames, candles and a small accent table can do a good job in making it look better.

The good thing about accessorizing a room is that you will never run out of choices. You can find a lot of items that you can use to accessorize your home including lighting fixtures or lamps to make it look more appealing and elegant.

Step #4: Personalize the room

Another vital step in any room makeover project is to integrate your unique personality into it. If you have a more laid-back personality, then make the room more personal by adding classical designs. If you are more outspoken or your personality is more on the modern side, then modern designs are perfect for the room. Be creative when integrating items that will represent your unique personality in a room's design.

Step #5: Add finishing touches

The last step in a room makeover is to add finishing touches. These finishing touches usually include furniture items and other accessories. The good thing is that you do not have to spend a fortune when buying furniture pieces and other room accessories. You can actually find bargained items or visit garage sales.

Additional decorations also fall under the category of finishing touches. These usually include additional lighting, flowers that perfectly blend with the overall theme and unique paintings.

Chapter 4: Working with Color Dynamics

When designing the interiors of your home, knowledge about color dynamics is a must. This is crucial in ensuring that you choose the right colors that perfectly blend with each other. Learning the basics of creating the best color flow and dynamics is the key to ensuring that your home brings out a more harmonious atmosphere.

The specific way interior decorators integrate light and color with space and form profoundly influence interior environments, as well as their overall design. It is also crucial to note that in this increasingly global and fast-paced world, new technologies in the field of lighting can actually change the way people view light and color, and eventually their interrelationships with the interior space. This is the main reason why some people tend to alter their choices when making light and color decisions.

Color dynamics is important in interior design because a strong knowledge about this field can help you fully understand the essence of every color, making it possible for you to renew your ability of seeing the world in a brighter and fresher perspective. To give you an idea about how to choose the right color dynamics, color scheme and color flow for your interior decorating project, consider keeping in mind the tips and factors mentioned in this chapter.

Consider lighting

Lighting is one of the most vital factors to consider when planning to choose the best color dynamics, scheme and flow for an interior design. Note that colors are reflections of light. This explains why the amount and kind of light used in a particular room can significantly affect color scheme. A wise tip is to experiment the way natural light or the light from recessed fixtures or lamps can affect different items and elements in a room such as furniture, paint, fabric and surfaces. Make sure that your chosen color blend well with the mentioned elements.

When on the stage of choosing the best color scheme for a specific room in your home, take time to examine the space during the day. Take note of the way shifting light influences it. For instance, if your room only has Northern exposure, then it is most likely that it will receive less daylight in comparison to your other rooms. In this case, consider choosing a warmer color palette as this is effective in softening shadows. Warm colors also react nicely to extra hours of artificial light.

If you are choosing colors for a room designed for use after sunset or before sunrise, then consider basing your colors on the artificial light used in that particular room. It is also important to note that colors with shades of white have the tendency of reflecting the hues surrounding them. For instance, a white wall will most likely reflect the colors of your furnishings, carpet and ceiling.

Use darker and lighter shades of one color in your home

This particular tip can help in creating a nice color flow. Think about how you plan to transition the colors from one room to another. You can seek the aid of a fan deck which many people consider as an indispensable tool when it comes to choosing the best shades for an interior design project.

Another tip in this category is to choose colors that have the same undertones. This is helpful in creating continuity and consistency.

You should also check out the existing furniture items in your home, so you can get an inspiration when it comes to choosing the best color dynamics and flow. Check out the artwork, fabrics, your favorite accessories, and other pieces of furniture inside your home so you can pick the right color combinations.

Choose the best hue for an open floor plan

If you have an open floor plan, then you may find the process of choosing the right colors for it tricky and challenging. The good news is that there are a few tips to guide you in this case. The first one is to allow the architectural plan to guide you. Find out if there are any transition areas or corners that will let you naturally start and stop a wall treatment like wallpapers or a paint color.

Another useful tip is to use monochromatic schemes. You can use this in changing the value of colors from one space to another. You can also take advantage of molding. Use the molding to delineate space. A 3-color scheme is also a good choice. This involves using a color on the walls, another hue on the trim and another one on your ceilings.

Benefits of Choosing the Right Color Dynamics

Choosing the right colors is crucial in transforming it into the kind of place that you want it to be. Note that the right color dynamics can unite even the most distinct furniture styles. You can also add color to your interior design to renew outdated and worn furniture. It enlivens the style of your home and make it look fresher and more attractive.

Another benefit of adding color is that it manipulates the space. You can turn a small room into a larger one just by using light colors. On the other hand, a large room will also look a bit smaller if you use dark hues for its walls. You can also visually raise a low ceiling by adding light colors.

Chapter 5: How to Best Utilize Textures?

One of the most vital elements in interior design is texture. The main reason is that it can add a distinct and unique dimension to your living space. This chapter will cover a few tips on effectively varying and balancing the textures in your interior decorating scheme.

Decorate your interior walls

Deciding to decorate your walls makes it possible to integrate texture into your living space. You can actually use a number of materials in decorating the walls, with each one having a positive impact in the overall mood of the room. One of these materials is the wallpaper which is ideal in covering drywalls because of the ease of its application and the fact that it is not permanent. Textured or patterned wallpapers can also add more flair to your walls. Just make sure that you take extreme caution when moving furniture and fixtures and hanging paintings so as not to damage the wallpapers.

You can also decorate your walls with wooden panels. The good thing about wooden panels is that they can transform any room into a timeless and cozy place. Try decorating the walls of your home office or bedroom with wall panels to make the atmosphere more inviting and warmer.

If you are looking for an inexpensive way to decorate your walls, then go for paint. Aside from being versatile, paint is also affordable. You can apply paint to create a wide range of distinct textures. You may also add face brick into your walls to make it more rustic and warmer.

Flooring

It is also possible to add texture into your home by choosing the right flooring. You can pick carpets that add a more luxurious appeal to your home. Soft and thick carpets are ideal for living rooms and bedrooms. You may also choose to install neutral carpets because these are simple, yet functional. Wooden and tile flooring are also among your best choices. Just make sure that your choice perfectly suits the overall theme of your home and showcases the kind of texture that you want it to present.

Add furniture and furnishings

Playing with different texture combinations is also possible by adding furniture and furnishings. Use your creativity when choosing furniture items to ensure that your desired texture will come out. It is also crucial to consider the mood of each room before buying furniture. For instance, if you want a cozy living room, then it is advisable to choose soft, wood and leather furnishings. You can also introduce texture into the overall interior design without spending a lot of money by adding soft furnishings including curtains, rugs and cushions.

Importance of Texture

Texture plays a lot of important roles in interior design. One vital role that it plays is it adds dimension and life to a room. Note that a room without texture will most likely appear boring and flat. Texture can also help you create a room which is full of character. Texture also enhances the features of a room. For instance, adding furnishings that feature shiny and smooth finishes into a dark and small room can help the space bring out a reflective quality and natural light.

Chapter 6: The Best Method for Designing a Room's Theme

The best method to design a room's theme is to be familiar about the basics of the most commonly used room themes at present. It is best if you have a strong knowledge about these themes, so you will be able to make a choice based on the current arrangements of your home and other items that go with it.

Minimalist Theme

The main idea behind the minimalist theme is to achieve simplicity by stripping everything down to the essential quality. This means that any unnecessary items are not welcome in minimalism. A minimalist design consists of only the most vital elements. Note, however, that this theme is not without any ornamentation. The concept is to reduce the design to the point that you cannot remove anything from it because all that are in there are essential. As a guide, the primary characteristics of the minimalist design are blue or white lighting, cool colors, large open spaces but with minimum and essential furniture only, features natural light and reduced to the ideal quantity.

Classic Theme

The classic interior design refers to the more refined and developed style. This style is also rich in details that are usually noticeable in the lighting, prints, sets and the structure of furniture items used. This theme is also based on symmetry, balance and order that perfectly complement the ideals of the Roman and Greek empires. One of the elements in this theme is the focal point. It uses focal point as a means of achieving visual balance.

It also makes use of color palettes inspired by nature. You can find a variety of greens, browns, blues, yellows and muted and softer colors such as pink, gray and terracotta in a lot of classic homes. If you want to accent the theme with whites, then consider picking off-white, especially if you plan to stick to the authentic classical style. You may also pick bright white in case you want it to feature a more contemporary feel.

Modern Theme

The modern theme usually comes with clean lines and emphasizes on functionality. It avoids using excessive decorative elements and accessories. While others may feel that the modern theme is too simple and a bit cold, note that it can still bring out a sense of simplicity and calmness in your home, if the design is well-planned. This is perfect for apartments and homes with small spaces because it can maximize the space while also creating an impression of a larger room. Bold geometrical forms, polished finishes, neutral colors with single bold hues as accents, asymmetrical balance and minimal texture are also among the features that can distinguish modern homes.

Modern Minimalist Theme

The modern minimalist features simplicity and extreme accuracy. It emphasizes on simplicity, so you can expect your home to have features and accessories that are not too much. It may use dull or bright colors, but the result is a more calming and peaceful atmosphere. This style also often makes use of geometric shapes like round, rectangular and square. It has clean surfaces with minimal to zero details and scenery. It is ideal for you if you want a more simplified version of a home.

Retro

It mimics the theme or style during the 50s, 60s and 70s. During that period, people started to anticipate that new designs will come. Today, many homes use the retro theme. It makes use of old designs, but with modern twists. The theme is usually characterized by an eclectic combination of new forms and old styles, or new forms that feature old finishes and materials. You can also find prints featuring geometric shapes and lines in this theme.

Contemporary Style

Contemporary style refers to trendy themes and appearances that are only in style at a current moment. One good thing about this style is that it is comfortable and inviting and devoid of clutter. Its main identifying feature is the line, which you can use by adding bold color blocks, linear wooden floor, square-edged furniture, bare windows and high ceilings. If you plan to choose the contemporary style, then keep in mind that furniture pieces with clean, smooth and geometric shapes are essential.

Chapter 7: Window Treatments

Window treatments are essential in interior design because aside from serving as window coverings, you can also use them to enhance the style and functionality of your windows. These window treatments play a number of roles including providing your needed privacy, controlling light, adding style and appeal to a room decoration and providing enough insulation. They can also offer you protection against the heat of the sun. If you are on the stage of choosing window treatments, then this chapter will be helpful for you as it provides different window treatment types and trends.

Tent-flap panels

This is the ideal window treatment for you if you want one which can protect you from the howling winter winds or the sweltering sunlight. These treatments will be applied within each window's frame, thereby providing enough room insulation. The panels can also provide clean lines that actually look appealing whether you close or open them based on your privacy needs and the current weather condition.

Pleated panels

Double-hung pleated panels work as effective window treatments because these showcase elegance and functionality in a more straightforward manner. If you plan to use the pleated panels, then you can actually create a more decorative and formal statement by adding angular valance. Keep it pleated to imitate the elegant and sophisticated jabots. However, if you want a more laid-back appeal, then you can use top panels featuring a flouncy, scalloped valance.

Luxury Fabrics

The use of luxury fabrics is a popular trend in the field of window treatments at present. You can actually pick velvets, silks, leather, fur, damasks and suede. The overall design actually emphasizes on simplicity. Despite that, a lot of interior designers believe that this trend will continue to be popular for a long time and is ideal for those who want luxury and embellishment. Interior decorators also say that this trend usually come along with lavish embellishments, beaded tassels, and sparkling crystal visible on each element of a window.

Sleek and Simple Lines

Another window treatment trend is the use of sleek and simple lines. This trend tends to dominate the window fashion industry from the flowing drapes up to the chrome decorative hardware. One reason why sleek and simple silhouettes and lines for windows gained popularity is that it provides a more modern and cleaner look not only to the window, but also to the entire room.

One way to obtain streamlined window treatments under this trend quickly is to use the panel-track system. This refers to wooden-wood or fabric panels that you can use not only on windows, but also in doors and as room dividers. Using the panel-track system as window treatment can also provide a European or contemporary look.

Silk Panels

While the silk panel is a costlier option when compared to other types of window treatments, you will realize that it is worth it considering the luxury and shine that the fabric showcases. It can bring life to an otherwise dull room. You can choose from a number of colors and from embroidered and plaid silks.

Whether you choose the types of window treatments mentioned here or the curtains, sheers, shutters, blinds and drapes, rest assured that these materials can effectively perform their function of adding a more aesthetic appeal to your home. Just make sure that you take good care of your chosen window treatments by maintaining and cleaning them properly, so they will last for a long time.

Chapter 8: Lighting and Ambiance Fundamentals

Lighting is another of the most important element in interior design. One purpose of installing the right lighting in interior design is for effective color management. Note that the kind of light that you use can either subtract from or add to the overall color of a particular surface or room. The light reflected off the walls and surfaces can also create an illusion of space.

If you want to soften the colors that you use in your wall, then consider installing directional lighting. An example of this is the track light. You can also install the recessed can lighting. It comes with a downward and soft glow, which is capable of illuminating the floors. If you want ambient illumination, then wall lighting or lights installed from the center of a room are your best choices. Your choice of light can greatly influence how dark or light a colored part of your home can be.

Another reason why lighting is important in interior design is its functionality. You should choose a lighting with a purpose, or else it will just end up wasting your electricity. For instance, chandeliers are usually found in open and large rooms, entryways and foyers not only because they are designed to be placed there, but also because of their ability to offer excellent illumination.

During the selection process, it is best to take into full consideration the style of light that you want. This helps in ensuring that you will receive the best luminescent or directional type for your chosen setting. Check out task-specific lighting options for work areas since these often require more functionality than illumination.

The right choice of light can also create the ambiance that you want your home to showcase. The good news is that both artificial and natural lights are effective in creating the illusion of space. If you have a darker room, for instance, then you have to look for a way to let full-spectrum natural light flow. Insufficient lighting can make the room feel and look cramped. Close-proximity furniture arrangements will also worsen the case.

If it is impossible for natural light to brighten a room, then central-hanging lights, wall sconces and corner lamps are best to choose. These artificial source of light can brighten the room while also creating the illusion of a larger space. However, it is still best to choose natural lighting over man-made ones because the former is capable of bringing out the best out of the colors used in a room.

Natural light also enhances visual space because of its ability to bounce off reflective surfaces. If you want to welcome natural light in the room, then consider having large windows or skylights. You may also choose sheer curtains and drapes. This can maximize the amount of light that enters through the window.

When making your choice, it is advisable to factor in the specific activities that often take place inside the room. You also need to consider the ambiance or mood that you want the room to deliver. Another factor to consider is the specific elements that you want to either hide or highlight.

Chapter 9: The Psychology of How a Room Makes you Feel

A well-designed room with the right colors can stimulate your mood. This is the main reason why interior designing should be carefully thought out. A messy room with poor design and color combinations can negatively affect your mood. To understand the psychology of how a room can make you feel, this chapter will cover a few colors usually used in a room and the effects of each one to the mood of a person.

Red

Red is a good choice if you want to raise the energy level of a room. Choose this color for your interior design project especially if you plan on stirring up excitement especially at night. Red is also a good choice for your dining and living room if you want to draw people together while also stimulating conversation. The color also leaves a strong impression if used in the entryway. Note, however, that it is not ideal for bedrooms since it is too stimulating. You may find it hard to sleep at night if your room is painted red since it has the tendency of raising your energy levels.

Yellow

Yellow is ideal for dining rooms, bathrooms and kitchens since these rooms require a happy color that is both uplifting and energizing. Yellow signifies happiness and captures the joy and beauty of the sun. You can also use yellow in small spaces and in halls since it is welcoming and can make the areas feel expansive. However, when designing a room, yellow is not ideal as a main color scheme. The reason is that some studies show that a yellow interior can cause most people to quickly lose their temper. You can still use this color, but only in lighter shades and not as the primary color of the room.

Blue

Blue is a color often associated to bringing down blood pressure and slowing heart and respiration rate. This is the main reason why many people find blue as serene, calming and relaxing. These qualities make the color ideal for bathrooms and bedrooms. However, take note that pastel blue which may look nice on a paint chip may be unpleasantly chilly when applied on furnishings and walls. This holds true for areas that receive less natural light.

If you plan to use light blue in your interior design project, then consider balancing it by using warm colors for fabrics and furnishings. You should also use warmer blues like periwinkles and bright blues like turquoise and cerulean if you want to stimulate relaxation in social settings such as in large kitchens, living rooms and family rooms.

Green

Many consider green as the most refreshing color. Green is also versatile that it can suit almost all rooms in your home. When applied in the kitchen, it can help cool things down. If applied in the living or family room, the color can stimulate everyone to unwind while still providing enough warmth for togetherness and comfort. You can also use it as the primary color for your interior designing project because of its calming effect. It is capable of relieving stress and making people feel relaxed.

Neutral Colors

Neutral colors include brown, white, gray and black, all of which are extremely important in an interior designer or decorator's tool kit. While the neutral color schemes have the tendency of falling in an out of the trend, their flexibility is still imminent, so expect to be able to use them regardless of the trend.

How you design a room, as well as its color, has a great effect on your mood. This is the main reason why you have to give interior designing a careful thought. Plan everything. Choose the right color scheme and theme and make sure that your choice fits your personality and lifestyle, as well as those of the people living with you. This will surely help you enjoy the results of your interior designing project.

Chapter 10: Common Modern Decorating Styles

Modern interior decoration reflects the modern art movement in a home's interior. There are several governing modern decorating styles at present. Modernism, when applied to interior design, rejects the ornate flourishes usually seen in other styles and designs such as those found in the Renaissance, Victorian and Gothic themes. Some of the most commonly used modern interior decorating styles at present are included in this chapter.

Use of Metal

Designs made from stainless steel and chrome are common in modern homes. It does away with the conventional metal details such as wrought iron and this works in creating polished and clean metals for living spaces. You can also see chrome and stainless steel used in various furniture and furnishings in modern homes like the exposed part of a chair's frame and the legs of a table. Chrome is also usually used in a number of useful accessories in modern homes including the railings, door knobs, lamps, faucets and cabinet handles.

Minimal clutter

Common modern decorating styles also have minimal to zero clutter. This makes the modern styles somewhat connected to the minimalist approach. In modern interior decorating, clutter specifically means accessories, and unnecessary ones at that. In other words, modern homes are devoid of unnecessary accessories including excessive number of vases, throw pillows, collections, blankets and rugs. It also eliminates unnecessary items such as unused electronics, books and keepsakes from sight. These are stored in a closet or cabinet.

Use of built-in shelves

Some modern decorating styles use built-in shelves to show that it is possible to display your personal items such as collectibles and pottery without adding too much clutter in your living room or in any other part of your home. One way to use built-in shelves without going beyond the principles of modern interior design is to spot lit them from within. This is a good way of showcasing the contents of the built-in shelves. Mimicking the lines seen in the main parts of the home can also help.

Modern kitchens

If you want your kitchen to have a modern theme, then it is advisable to install cabinets and counters that feature clean lines and are devoid of raised panels and decorative edges. Another tip is to repeat sharp lines all throughout the kitchen backsplash. The entire room should also showcase one, monochromatic color.

Bolder accent colors

Another unique modern decorating style is the use of bolder accent colors. Most homes that apply the modern theme utilize neutral shades and colors of black and white. Bold colors that often refer to primary colors serve as accents that aim to emphasize the focal points in your home while also breaking up the neutral colors. A few examples of items that allow you to apply bold accent colors in a modern interior design project effectively are abstract wall arts, bold-colored throw rugs and pillows, accent wall, one piece of bold-colored furniture like a red sofa made from leather.

Chapter 11: Designing for Feng Shui

If you believe in Feng Shui, then be aware that there are a few interior decorating tips that will allow you to stick to its principles. Try improving the flow of energy to your living space through the Feng Shui designing principles mentioned in this chapter.

Place furniture items in the right position

Place your furniture in an area where free passage to the room is not restricted. This can prevent you from restricting the flow of positive energy and luck. Your furniture should also be positioned in such a way that people can sit on it with their backs against the wall.

Hang mirrors

In Feng Shui, mirrors are important items because many believe that these can reflect positive energy. Mirrors are also said to be effective in preventing negative energy from flowing inside the home. Note, however, that it is not advisable to hang a mirror in a place where it faces the front door since it may drive positive energy away from the house.

Don't add sharp corners and lines

In Feng Shui, roundness is more preferable. Sharp corners should be avoided since these are believed to produce negative energy. If possible, avoid pointing any corners to chairs and beds since this position can prevent relaxation and calmness.

Stock up on Feng Shui items for wealth and abundance

If you want to stimulate abundance in all aspects of your life, then consider adding and placing colors and items recommended by the Feng Shui principles at the far left corner of your home or room. Items believed to increase prosperity in Feng Shui are valuable or expensive possessions like sculpture, coins, crystals and works of art, water features like fish tanks, fountains and waterfalls, fresh plants with purple, red or blue flowers, artwork and pictures that represent your desired possessions like jewelries or car, wind chimes and healthy plants including those with coin-shaped and round leaves.

Integrate tones and items that attract reputation and fame

Feng Shui also recommends owning and placing a few items in certain parts of the home to those who wish to attract opportunities, reputation and fame. These include red and pink items, candles, fireplaces, lamps, pictures of people you admire or you wish to emulate, arrangements in groups of 9, electrical equipment and any items connected to animals including leather, wool, silk, bird feeders and animals prints.

Install a water feature in your home

A water feature is vital in Feng Shui because it signifies one of its features, which is wind water. Installing anything that features water in your home can stimulate harmony, peace and relaxation.

Chapter 12: Designing for Functionality

Interior design does not solely focus on the aesthetics. It also puts a lot of emphasis on functionality. This means that you cannot expect your interior design project to be successful if you only focus on how you can make your home attractive. To guarantee success in interior design, it is advisable to learn a few tips on how to design for functionality.

Your plan should have a purpose

Never ever start to design a living space or a particular area in your home unless you know exactly its intended purpose. This means that you have to create a plan that talks about the purpose of the space before you ever start to decide on trim and color schemes. Note that not understanding the main purpose of a specific room may only cause you to fail in putting and combining the right accent pieces. Creating an interior design plan that has a clear purpose can help you look at even the tiniest details of the project. This will surely result to the best room design.

Have a functional layout

You cannot start your interior design project without the room's functional layout. This is where you can input furniture and room measurements and start playing with your options to determine the most optimal choice. Design your room first with the help of a layout to avoid the burden of moving heavy furniture from one place to another, only to end up failing to get your desired layout. It should also be noted that your home's functionality is dependent on your lifestyle and preferences. You cannot expect the layout of another home to also work for you. You have to consider a lot about your personality to achieve better results.

Consider the cost

Designing for functionality also requires you to keep in mind the cost of the entire project. Note that wasteful design is a common occurrence in the interior design industry and this often happens to people who did not develop a proper floor plan or design. Think of the cost that you will most likely spend on the overall design. Start to visit several stores that offer the items that you need, so you can start comparing prices. It is also advisable to set a budget and commit to sticking to it to avoid splurging your money over something which you cannot use for a long time.

Find functional decorative objects

You should spend your money over decorative objects that improve not only the attractiveness of your home, but also its functionality. Try to look for budget-friendly decorative items that you can really use at home. If you are still new in the field of interior design, then you can always gain help by browsing through interior showrooms and magazines. Just make sure that you do not end up buying impulsively.

Integrate layers

Integrating layers into your home's interiors is useful for visual warmth and comfort. Layering certain elements in your home such as your area rug, pillows and carpet can help you develop a cozy atmosphere and well-decorated aesthetic.

Add greens

Many people fail to think about adding plants into their homes, believing that they have already achieved the best design. However, not adding even just one plant inside your home is a huge interior design mistake. Adding just one plant can add warmth to your home and increase its natural element.

Chapter 13: The Best Online Resources for Interior Design

Whether you are still a starter or already have a lot of experience in interior design, it pays to increase your knowledge about this field continuously. Fortunately, you can gain easy access to some of the best online resources for relevant and up to date interior design information. Some of these resources are mentioned in this chapter.

Houzz.com

This site has the largest collection of interior design and home improvement ideas online. You can find numerous designs that will suit each room in your home just by visiting the site. It also has a huge database that store millions of interior decorating pictures. You will surely find a lot of inspiration for your interior design project through this site.

Icreatived.com

This is another popular website that provides a lot of information regarding interior design. It is a high-end, browsable blog that offers information about the trendiest and high-concept interiors. Visiting this site will surely help fill your mind with useful information about how to go on designing your home.

Wowhaus.co.uk

You can also visit this popular site to gain inspiration when creating an interior design. This site features interesting houses every day, whether these fall under the modern, retro, art deco, contemporary or minimalistic style. You will surely gain ideas from their featured houses.

Roomenvy.co.uk

This is a blog where you can find a lot of useful information about interesting interior decorating styles. It also features interesting room design concepts, cool kitchens and other interesting stuff about interior design to guide both amateur and experienced designers.

Designspiration.net

This site puts interesting homes on the spotlight by featuring them complete with concepts and pictures. Among the featured homes are those that were transformed by leading designers and architects in the world.

Conclusion

Thank you again for downloading this book!

I hope this book was able to provide you with ample information about interior design. Interior decorating may be an overwhelming endeavor considering the many factors that you have to consider. One poorly designed element in a home's interior can greatly affect the overall appeal of the structure so you have to be really careful. However, with proper knowledge, you will be able to handle all the challenges linked to interior design.

The next step is to apply what this book taught you in your next interior decorating project. This book is extensive enough that it covers a number of vital aspects related to the field. By keeping in mind all the information that this book offered you, you will surely be able to turn a room or a home into an amazing place.

Finally, if you enjoyed this book, please take the time to share your thoughts and post a review on Amazon. It'd be greatly appreciated!

Thank you and good luck!